Poetry and Business

Edited by

Jonathan Cook

"Without meaning, work is pain and we must be bludgeoned
into it." - George S. Odiome

TO SUBMIT

Poetry and Business is published once a year, on Groundhog's Day. For submission guidelines, visit PoetryAndBusiness.com

CONTENTS

DOWN TO BUSINESS

This is the first issue of Poetry and Business, a journal of verse dedicated to the significant but neglected territory where metaphor and marketing intermingle.

It is published on Groundhog's Day, on the threshold between recession and growth, where an oracle of underground wealth emerges to the edge of its cave, a small bear ready to steal the bulls of Apollo, forecasting marketplace performance with a combination of confidence and a poor track record that could earn it a place on CNBC's schedule, if only it could speak in more than a grunt.

As poetry speaks, it moves between the world of deep roots and the bright, busy surface. Business trades in the same shift, exchanging our accumulated stores of sacrifice and unaccounted time for the clear realities above.

As poets of business, we labor to mine the hidden value in tunnels that twist in dimensions unimaginable to those standing on the flat market landscape shown on the maps. It is an unnatural commerce, between unfriendly realms, but where others refuse to look, we find fruitful meaning.

When hibernation ends, we seek meaning on the outside, only finding our shadows when we come forth from the depths. Emerge with us.

THE METAPHOR OF MONEY

It is typical for editors of poetry journals to begin with a summary for readers of what they can expect in the pages to follow, providing their own interpretations, as if to prove that the poems have, in fact, been read and understood. This habit, after years of processing poems merely as material for homework assignments, demands that poems will no longer simply be experienced, but must be explained.

I'll provide no such reiteration, presuming that you're capable of encountering the poems on their own terms. What mysteries remain after you read them may guide you more than the words themselves.

This journal has not been assembled, however, as a collection of poetry for its own sake. Its purpose is implied by its name. The mission of Poetry and Business is to cross the sparsely-populated borderlands that lie between the territories occupied, in comfortable separation, by business people and by poets.

Poets and people in business tend not to be very fond of each other. Business professionals usually scoff at poets as impractical, detached from the struggles with profit and loss that drive the production of material worth or lead to ruin. Poets, for their part, typically dismiss people in business as superficial sellouts who never pause to consider the deeper significance of life.

Oscar Wilde depicted this mutual antipathy over a hundred years ago, casting the capitalist as a cynic who "knows the price of everything but the value of nothing", and the "sentimentalist" as someone who "sees an absurd value in everything and doesn't know the market price of any single thing". The tragedy at the heart of this longstanding conflict is that the partisans of poetry and business are both so consumed by the importance of their own perspectives that they are unable to perceive what they share in common.

Poets deal in metaphor, the subtle speech that directs attention to one thing by pointing at another. Symbolism is thick in human life, however. Poetry that matters comes from the search for unexpected connections, not from the obvious links. It's easy to draw a comparison between love and a flower. It takes a skillful poet to find romance in a performance review.

In our culture, it's marketers who usually take on these more challenging tasks of poetic exploration. They work with the exchange of unlike things: A series of tasks exchanged for a month of time, exchanged for a story, exchanged for a car, exchanged for a journey, exchanged for an object found at the end of the road, displayed on a shelf in the office where a new set of tasks will be assigned.

Every commercial interaction is a poetic act, with a transformative trick of translation from material to ethereal, condensed back into material again. Yes, marketers perform these acts of poetry in exchange for money, rather than from sincere feeling or inspiration in the moment. Does that make their poetry less poetic?

As a journalist might say, follow the money.

When people in business work in exchange for money, they do so out of devotion, to their work, to the important people in their lives, or to a future with better odds. Their work is a sacrifice in exchange for money, and sacrifice is much more than an act of surrender. Sacrifice is an act full of symbolic meaning, through which mundane objects are transformed into tools of sacred power.

In our culture, money is the most sacred object of all. It is a transcendental medium for symbolic magic. It can turn an hour into a sandwich, an idea into a pair of shoes.

The metaphorical power of money has shaped human lives for over a hundred generations, going back all the way to the ancient Greeks and their discovery of metallic alchemy. Learning how to melt cold, hard materials from the ground into little amulets of power, they became able to engage in acts of metaphoric trade over huge distances.

So, magical transformation became associated with travel as well.

The potency of these meanings became embodied in one symbol:

Try, for a moment, to put aside all the associations you have with this symbol. Look past the "dollar sign". Try to see what it actually looks like, and you'll realize that it's not just a random shape, that it's more than just an S with a line through it.

It looks like nothing so much as a snake, curving its way around a stick. It looks remarkably like this:

It may occur to you that you've seen another symbol like this, perhaps on the side of an ambulance. In this version, this symbol is known as the rod of Asclepius, which represents the profession of medicine.

A snake on a stick was a widespread symbol in the ancient world, believed to confer mystical power. In fact, this symbol is the original magic wand. The snake that slides up and down its length only disappeared from the wand of power in relatively recent times. Harry Potter and his friend, it turns out, were playing with snakes right along with Salazar Slytherin, only theirs were metaphorical, and invisible.

The symbol was found even over in India, where the vision of a snake rising up a stick was used as a metaphor for the human spine, with the chakras of power located at every turning of the serpent, with spiritual enlightenment waiting at the very top.

The version of the symbol that you see here, however, isn't from India. It's the caduceus, the symbol of the deity known to the Greeks as Hermes, and given the name Mercury by the Romans. Mercury, of course, is more than just the name of an ancient Roman divinity. It's also the name of a singular metal, the only one that is liquid at room temperature.

Thus, we return to the ancient fascination with metal, and with money. Mercury represents fluidity, as shown in the writhing, wave-like form of the snake. A metal in a liquid state represents pure potential for transformation, sliding into a new form, such as the form of a coin, when it is poured into the proper mold. A coin, therefore, represents liquid wealth made tangible. Its value, at least in the ancient world, came from the fact that it could be melted down over and over again and given new form.

That power for transformation is what the caduceus, and the divinity it represents, is all about. The two snakes of the caduceus symbolize the fundamental opposites of human existence: Male and female, light and dark, life and death, abundance and poverty, qualitative and quantitative knowledge… and, we could say, poetry and business. The important thing about the serpents of the caduceus is that they trade places, crossing over the seemingly firm boundary represented by the central staff, so that dark becomes light, death becomes life, and poverty becomes abundance.

So, too, can business become poetry, and poetry become business.

The curve of the snake on the caduceus, and on the dollar sign, recalls the shape of the winding road traveled by traders, moving along borderlands from town to town. Trade first took place along the borders of territories controlled by opposing groups who would, ordinarily, engage in battle when they met.

At special places, marked by piles of stones, different rules applied. At these places, enemies could leave each other items for trade, with the understanding that any person discovered near these stone caches would be protected from physical violence, even if they were caught stealing across enemy territory. Eventually, the paths between these stone trading posts became the routes used by traders to pass from community to community. The piles of stones grew into shrines to Mercury.

In the ancient world, money wasn't just a tool, and commerce was much more than a rational system for economic development. Mercury was the divine spirit of commerce. The Latin meaning of com-merx, after all, was to be with Mercury. Because traders were the bearers of news from foreign realms, Mercury became the patron of travel and communication as well. Given the ability of coins to shift value easily from one form to another, Mercury also became the god of ritual, the symbolic means of identity transformation older than humanity itself.

Poetry and Business is published on Groundhog's Day in observance of the fact that it was Mercury who, once a year, descended down through a hole in the ground into the underworld to take Persephone, the goddess of springtime and daughter of agricultural prosperity, away from Pluto, who had hoarded her like a dead treasure in the dark. The Groundhog's Day we celebrate today is a relic of this ancient mystery. Only Mercury could cross the border between the two realms of death and life, without seeking to possess the treasure for himself, only helping it to move back and forth, a snake crawling over a stick.

So it was that Mercury was also known as the patron of thieves. In our own time, we wonder how Mercury could simultaneously be the patron of commerce and of criminals, but in ancient Greek culture, trade with coins was a radical departure from the region's traditional economic culture, which was controlled by a few noble families through a process of gift exchange.

Traders traveling under the mantle of Mercury were threats to the status of these powerful nobles, stealing across borders and enabling ordinary people to exchange goods through the use of shiny metal discs. The nobles denounced these traders as thieves, and called their patron the god of thieves. Like the god of the underworld, these plutocrats wanted to hoard their wealth, and were afraid of having it stolen away by the devotees of Mercury.

These aristocrats were responsible for giving marketing its reputation as a wicked craft. It is because of their hatred of traders that money was recast as a corrupting influence. Echoes of this old hostility inform the present day charges by poets against people who engage in creative communication in exchange for money, accusing them of being superficial and not worthy of trust.

Of course, there's some truth to these charges. Money, and the work we do with it, can become a superficial attachment. When we think of money as a treasure to be counted and kept, rather than a means of empowering exchange, we take on the character of Pluto, begrudging Mercury his warm and fuzzy ambiguity. Instead of recognizing a sale as a cherished moment of mutual sacrifice, rich in meaning for all involved, we literally discount the significance of commerce, trying to squeeze every last bit of value from it.

The need of a deeper aesthetic of business has never been greater. With the development of digital technology, business culture has increasingly become digital itself, unable to see beyond the apparently absolute distinctions between opposites such as zero and one. Big Data is a tool with astonishing power that large businesses would be unwise to ignore. However, the rapid growth of the algorithmic outlook without a counterbalancing growth in the organic, mythological side of business has led to an unprecedented disengagement from commercial culture on the part of consumers and marketers alike.

Poetry has its own problems. As poets have moved into the insulated settings of universities and creative writing programs, their work has tended to become more self-referential, detached from the passions that shape life outside of their classrooms. Unsure of how to communicate in a relevant way with the outside world, poets rarely take up the lyre of Mercury any more, but lean toward the Apollonian vanity it once tempered.

The ancient balance between Mercury and Pluto can be restored. The common ground between poets and traders can be found again. The purpose of Poetry and Business is to begin this project of reconciliation.

Poetry has a special power, as a subjective and qualitative form of communication, to bring the flexible, fluid movement of Mercury back to the commerce of our times, even as the inherently relevant symbolism of commerce brings poetry back in touch with the vital flow of contemporary culture.

As with trade, it will take two willing sides to make the deal work. David Whyte, a poet and corporate consultant, explains that "Whatever project, plan, or career you commit to, there will always be a deeper dynamic you discover inside, a promise larger than your original conception that in effect makes vows on your behalf and invites you to find a different kind of courage than you first intended." In business, people will need to look deeper to find the poetry within their work. Poets will need to pursue more authentic engagement as well, to find where their metaphors can gain purchase upon the world in ways that enable them to do work that matters.

The gift of a mercurial identity is liberation from singular attachment to any role. To pursue the path of commerce is to accept the role of making change. As followers of Mercury, we shape shift, dancing between the poses of business and poetry, stealing from each to enrich the other.

The following poems are an invitation to poets and marketers alike to cross the border that separates them, and to speak with one another in verse.

LISA TIMPF

OUT THE WINDOW

Fortunately, there were no windows, then
not close enough, anyway
to see the day's weather
indoors, the forecast
was for ongoing computer work
with a chance of meetings,
a constant high pressure system
and a possibility of emotional thunderstorms
the fronts waxing warm or cold
depending on the mood
and the weight of the wind,
that could crush you if you didn't keep your head down
sometimes
keeping one eye out for catastrophic weather
a shovel to hand for digging out
when things got tough
keeping the feelers out for
what was coming or might come,
that was the trick,
until you learned to read the business forecast
almost by osmosis

sometimes she would get out into the outside world
and blink in surprise
seeing the brightness and
feeling the warmth of the sun
on her untanned face.

NATHAN MASTERSON

COLLABORATION

The project manager I work with
always takes my first drafts.
I say to her, in the note I attach,
this is just a rough sketch.
Let's talk about it some more and see
where we can take it.
I click send, and the program I've got
on the computer I've got
that they say is designed for design,
makes it sound like this is an airplane
taking off,
ripping into the clouds
on a journey nearly into outer space
before it falls
to a place where the frequent flyers
exit briskly to complete their vital missions.
I never get a reply,
and in the workflow database
posted on the cloud
I see my contribution checked off.
When I see her coming
down along the side of the cubicle
risen under the square ceiling tiles
running away under parallel lines
to the horizon somewhere
beyond where they can be seen meeting
past the exit sign
at a point outside building C137
looping over and over again
through the wall
in formation
to create the appearance

of a single thing,
one soft body,
she merely says
thank you for your report,
and turns away briskly
to talk with the guy by the elevators.
They call him the wordsmith.

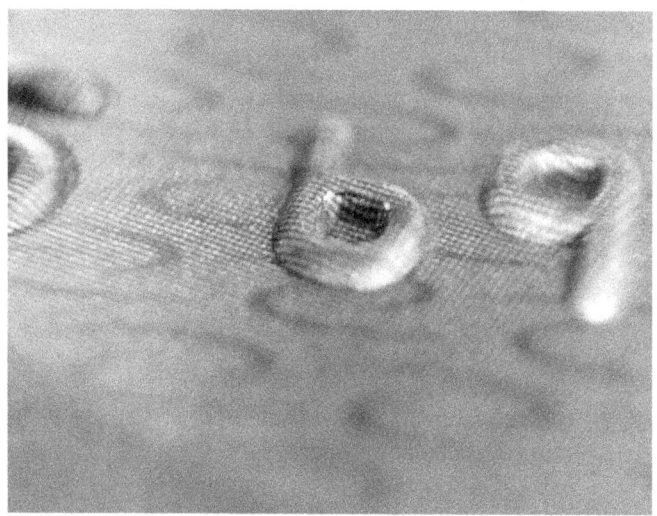

CRAIG MORITA

Midway along the journey of life,
I accepted this task
discounting leftovers
in the family business.
This year I approach
a bin of marshmallow trees,
wrapped in chocolate
wrapped in false metal foil
with my pistol of stickers
replacing yesterday's dollar
with today's 50 cents.
The next morning, a girl
wearing black against the grey
pauses by the display
only to say
"empty calories"
and move on.
Nobody fancies a holiday
the day after.

LISA TIMPF

THE SMELL OF COFFEE

In later years, the smell of coffee
would have a way of reminding her
of burning hot sand on the soles of bare fee
and the way the road would slip away
from under the back tire of your bike
out by the tall choke-cherry tree
that tree stood sentinel
near the fields where the tawny Clydesdale
would bunch his massive hindquarters
to overcome the inertia
of the tobacco boat
and jolt it forward
as its runners cast a smell of hot steel
into the hot air
while the primers endured the slaps
of the cold, dew-wet morning tobacco leaves
followed by the sweat-drenching warmth
of the August afternoons
as the day's humidity notched up
the smell of coffee reminds her of riding her bike
over the railway tracks that shimmered away
into the distance
pedaling into the kiln yard
through the orchard of ancient apple trees
that spilled their half-ripened fruit to the ground,
stopping to watch the ladies on the table gang-
her mother included--
weave the leaves, deft-handed
onto the wooden slats, then sent them up the
groaning elevator, where the kiln hanger
traversing the rafters with the grace of
trapeze artist, plucked the loaded sticks

just before they dropped off the end
and arranged them on the wooden beams
to allow the heat up, later, for curing
ah, but at break time, everything stopped
the primers, the table gang, the driver, the kiln hanger
hands dark and stiff with a coating of tobacco tar
reached for cookies, opened thermoses
to let forth a trickle of steam and the smell
of fresh, hot coffee
and now, when she cups her hand gently
around a mug of that same beverage
in a much cleaner cafeteria
decades and miles away
the aroma reminds her of those days
and links her to her childhood
providing a continuity
reminding her not to be afraid
to get her hands dirty.

MARINA HATSOPOULOS

REJECTION

I slip through the conference hall in my heels, waving to some venture capitalist buddies in back, but a guy in glasses corners me and pitches his startup. He's wearing a suit—rookie mistake—and says he'll sell his business in 18 months, probably to Google, for at least 20x. I wish it were as easy to delete a conversation in person as it is in email. I tell him I'm not interested. He has no clue how long it takes to build a technology business, and shows none of the commitment needed to handle the bumps in the road. It's grueling work, which is why I sold my business. It allowed me to start angel investing while pursuing my lifelong dream of publishing a novel.

During the conference, I check my overflowing inbox. I refine my rejection email to be clearer and more succinct, and I come up with a new filter—no social apps—which makes the process more efficient. If I'm not decisive, I'll drown under all the pitches. I like hardware startups, but searching for investments is like house-hunting; I may say I want a Cape, but then fall in love with a Colonial. At the end of the day, after all the analysis, it requires some blind faith and gut feel, because the risks are high and nothing is yet proven. In short, I have to get it.

Hidden in my inbox is an email from the literary agent who had shown interest in my novel. After so many rejections, I had finally found someone who liked my story about a woman leading a technology startup. This agent didn't think business was de-facto boring. She got it.

I'm so excited. I've been waiting for weeks to get her comments on my revisions. I open the email, but it's not pages of analysis like her last one. It's a rejection. A kick in my face.

I turn down and cover my eyes. It shouldn't be this

difficult. With millions of books on amazon, I only need one of them to be mine. I'm overwhelmed by my longing for readers; not the recognition, but the act of moving another person's mind. Maybe this is a sign that I should let the dream go. I've wasted ten years, struggling alone at my desk every day for hours, searching for words, sending my work out to the world over and over, and I've created nothing of value. I should stick with investing, where I can be the one doing the rejecting.

I wipe my nose as I stand up to leave, but before I escape, the entrepreneur returns.

"You guys were pioneers," he says. "It took the mass media—what—like fifteen years to discover 3D printing. Why'd you sell it?"

"I was burned out." Maybe we shouldn't have sold. I *was* somebody, and now what am I?

This guy's eyes light up when he explains his technology. His startup is risky and he hasn't even built a prototype. I prepare an explanation for why I won't invest, but I try to think of words to soften the message, like the agent did.

I remember now that he's emailed me several times. I want to reward him for his tenacity, tracking me down, so instead of walking away, I articulate the problems I see with his business model. He listens and takes notes. Maybe rejection is only the end for those who don't use the information to move forward.

"Everything takes a lot longer than you think," I say. "We had to rework the pitch, over and over. Our sales took over a year to close, which was scary; we really needed the cash."

"Why didn't you raise more money?"

"We got turned down by every VC in town and thought we'd have to fold. Dark days, but we trudged through until we found a speckle of light," I say.

He's taller than me, which feels incongruous with the power dynamics of the situation. He has to stand with his legs far apart to keep from stooping over.

"It's hard, but I love it," he smiles.

And I love writing. It's about creating something from a blank slate.

"Any advice?" he asks. It's code for asking if I want to invest.

"Stick with it. We never gave up when people said we had a crappy product."

The protagonist in my novel would never give up either. I'm going to write back to ask the agent for feedback.

To be honest, I'm not sure this all happened in one day, but, with so many rejections, who knows. What I learned about investing from being rejected as a writer was humility, respect and kindness. Even if I ultimately say no, I try to help out when I can. What I learned about writing from being pitched as an investor was that rejection is not the end. It doesn't mean there's nothing of value, but that more work may be needed. Pitching requires perseverance and blind faith that eventually someone will get it. The outcome is somewhat based on personal preference and fit, which makes it a game of numbers: you have to kiss a lot of frogs. But it's like falling in love; you only need one.

"Would you invest?" he asks, leaning in. This guy is fearless. He could be the next great CEO. He's exuding hope. I love that feeling and I want it back.

"Let's have coffee," I say. "I know an expert in the field who I'll introduce to you."

I shake his hand to leave. I need to sift through the database of agents to find five new names. After I re-work my manuscript, I'm going to send it out again.

This entrepreneur thinks I have power, but, even if I invest, my supporting role will fade to insignificance after a customer is consuming his product. In the end, he is the one with the power to make the world different than it was before, through his act of creation.

SARAH AYDOGDU

MILESTONE

There is no clear line to mark it
but those who know the trick
of trading places can follow
the path here in the marches
seeing a sign in a fallen scale
rubbed off against the edge
on either side while avoiding
the gaze of a shadow
pursuing another way
across this vibrating border.
We steal through this quietly together
seeking the same position
in sync out of sync
away from wide soldiers' roads
meeting the enemy with a sacrifice
of lost days tied up and placed
under a pile of stones
marking our mutual surrender in exchange
for a frozen flow of quicksilver
to be born through this passage
out of the night of being
all things and nothing emerging
into solid arrangement of purpose
falling into the shadow in which
we recognize finally what we had
hoped to become entering
foreign territory as from behind us
a flash of light bursts
off into the opposite
direction having ended this
encounter of customs
double crossed.

LANA BELLA

DEAR SUKI: LETTER F FOR FORWARD

Dear Suki: San Francisco, October 4th, briny air rises
as tremor of the sea coasts over Pier 39. Fingering the
cold, I pull my flesh deeper into the down-filled parka,
when the tiny furs on the dark undersides gently pull
this moment forward, as if to jog my mind of the path
that is always interconnecting between you and I. Dear
Suki, this brief afternoon at the wharf, I am just a lone
figure seen nipping on a bowl of bread chowder, sipping
a cold beer, savoring a handful of cigarettes; I remain
in such rhythm as long as I could, which isn't too long,
for my next destination is calling to me from the brink
of periphery. Though I must say most days are like that
when I travel for business, if I'm lucky, I would snatch
a brief solitary moment for myself among the locals, then
I would close my eyes in sleep over the Transpacific or
Transatlantic flight, thereupon I'd wake with you and I
brushing fingertips at airport terminals or me waiting
before the gate closes shut, leaving aerial kisses from
telephone booths around the world on your voicemail
as you quietly dream.

LEANN DVORKIN

EXECUTIVE

The grain between this table
and the empty blue ocean
is weather stained and pushed into dark furrows
by the invisible hand of a passing front
the tiny engines that produce its yield
bleached of their profitable color
unharvested you did not account
as you set out on your straight course
for the water hiding in this dry land
made of the illusion of its striving tops
growing from a sodden mat of last year's failures
ever falling ever rising you did not stop
when you felt the cold flowing over the tops
of your shoes but kept striding
leaving your mark on the field with every step
a shadow of ambition cast by broken stalks
until you found your final position
frozen within sight of your ship
almost its captain
by this time next year
your reaching arm will have
disappeared.

Issue 1 - 2016

TERRY BRIX

POETIC COEFFICIENT

Engineering, science, even going from diameters
to circumference needs dimensionless numbers.
Some have names like "!". No kilograms, ounces,
horse power, feet with all their branded baggage—
just ratios, fudge factors. There is relative volatility
in distillation—just the ratio of vapor & liquid
compositions in controlled experiments ending
in a number between 1.0 & 3.0 where one means
impossible to separate, 3.0 is anvil in bathtub easy.

Poets are finders of dimensionless numbers,
compare, heft images that aren't comparable.
Find a truth between sunset & sunburn,
link between a mountain & a molecule,
how a kiss is a head-on collision of two pasts.
How new granddaughter Clair is just as fragile
as an idea to make fragrances from turpentine.

How words, numbers circle my head like vultures
picking away at my old three-dimensional life.
Cubed constipated with $, %, £, kilowatts, ft2,
life becoming dimensionless coefficients
tacked on things held most dear to only me.

HARVEY JONES

WHERE CREDIT IS DUE

mirrors on the sides of these numbers
darkened as out fingers meet in mutual
sacrifice
the secret of my worth hidden within
this skin
pierced by a needle pointing true
north
following a code no one will bother
memorizing
an unread signature our wives and husbands
forge
on grocery runs seeking forgotten
ingredients
swiping a key to the lists of each
purchase
every hair stands to attention as I pass
checked
charged

SALLY CLARK

GETTING READY FOR WORK

A tight pair of jeans
keeps the bills from slipping out;

a dark t-shirt won't show
ketchup or beer or iced tea stains;

an apron full of pens, lots of pens,
to replace the ones she gives away,
but never gets back;

a thick skin to endure the kitchen's insults;

a fast smile for the customers
who think she wants to be here,

and a dream to keep in the back of her mind,
like a gift she'll save until later,
much later,
to open

APRIL ORKUDA

INDEPENDENT CONTRACTOR

Last night I dreamed
I wanted to be a folksinger
accompanying a respected local
guitarist I was on main street
at a festival in the evening
with 1000 stars on
the ground upside down
but I had only one song written
though I had plenty of time
to prepare so I stopped singing
and hit the tambourine for a while
and watched my brother play
familiar tunes I hadn't heard
for years until I was in
the back row of the crowd
that somehow I had never
left and walked over
to the unemployment line where I
work as a clerk
for 15 years pretending
I meant it all along
never applying
never filling out
the form.

ROGER HIGGINS

VITAL STATISTICS

Expect minus twenty-seven, feels like minus thirty-three,
I am decked out in thermals and multiple layers,
cheekbones feeling like thin glass
that would shatter at a touch.

And we are already below forecast
without counting the chill of a wind
piling blown snow to the rooflines of the few buildings,
the window glass displaying in strata
the past week's weather.

Vital statistics.
Thirty-six, thirty, thirty-five,
imitating the figure of a centrefold,
but these are the temperatures below zero
at breakfast, lunch and dinner.

**

In this the crews work
pouring concrete and erecting steel,
five weeks on so far, feels like twenty,
and chicken again in the mess tonight.

There are other vital statistics here.
This one has a daughter, sixteen with a habit,
this one a son aged eight, gone with his stepfather,
a mother BP seventy-five over fifty and failing fast,
a best friend who isn't returning messages any more,
and it's minus thirty-seven now on the gauge,
feels like minus forty-five,
nothing will keep them warm

and no way to get home for five more weeks.

**

Accidents happen too easily.
The incident rate is one point five,
productivity is down to zero point six,
the work is twelve percent behind schedule
and everything is on the critical path.
Vital statistics.
Three birthdays and two anniversaries missed this week,
eighteen emails about loneliness across time zones,
three supervisors went to town, got drunk, were fired,
eleven men did not return from field break.
The temperature is back up to minus thirty
but the wind is gusting to twenty knots, feels like minus forty.

**

My breath is icing on the window of the four-wheel drive.
I scrape at it with the loyalty card from a coffee shop somewhere,
perhaps the best value I will get from that card
although I would enjoy a cappuccino right now, dusted with cocoa.
My piss steams in the frozen outhouse,
horses stand like weather vanes to the wind.

EDITH OUVERT

PILGRIM

In the gas station, I see the same people every morning, lining up for the checkout counter.

There's a young man, in his twenties, who buys custard-filled doughnuts from a display saying they come from a local bakery, though they look the same as every other custard-filled doughnut I've ever seen in any gas station anywhere in the United States. They call them Boston Creme. My word processor wants to autocorrect the way I spell Creme, putting a French accent on it, but I'm pretty sure that nobody pronounces "Boston Creme" so that it rhymes with phlegm.

A young woman who I used to say looked like she was fresh out of high school buys a pack of menthol cigarettes along with a packet of flaming hot cheese snacks every morning. I stopped wondering to myself whether she is taking meth about two years ago.

My neighbor comes in, flips over the local newspaper to see what's below the big headlines, sniffs, shakes his head, and then puts it back on the rack, upside down. We never talk. We look at each other, but pretend not to see each other.

None of us ever talk to each other. Silence is the code of the gas station, broken only when our voices rasp, almost in apology, in response to the clerk's question, to say that no, we would like to use our bank cards as credit, not as debit to get cash back.

We are on the road, though we are temporarily in a gas station together, not far from home. The point is that we have entered the road, or perhaps we should say that we have allowed the road to enter us, to occupy us, to fill us up as if we are the empty tanks, filled with emptiness until we reach our destinations.

"A commute of a mile is a short ode," writes Glynn Young, author of Poetry At Work. I read that line a couple of months ago, but I had been feeling it for years, writing the poetry of my route to work in my mind from scratch every day.

The morning commute is what I think of when I think of driving the car, perhaps because the future does not call for my attention in the morning, distracting me from the present with promises of better times. The poem written in the morning is erased with the afternoon commute's fantasies of empty time that will, this time, be protected from the line of just this little thing first.

We commute apart together.

Back on the road, I look for the Bernie Sanders supporter, whose stickers also tell me that if there are no farms, there will be no food, and that I must not be paying attention, because I can't summon a feeling of genuine outrage anymore. I ask myself, what if I were to be outraged? Would it change anything? In the morning, I don't think so, but in the afternoon, I begin to suspect that my outrage could join with others', and then we'd all see the change we want to be in the world, but I also remember that I have to take care of just this little thing first.

Commuting, we leave behind last night's embarrassing surrender to wrinkled sheets left on the bed for a week longer than we planned, boxes of takeout food on top of Monday's stickie notes, and that new smartphone app that turns a game with sugary treats into a just this little thing first, only because it beeps at us in an optimistic way.

I've never read a poem about this life, though I see thousands moving in this same direction, silently with me. I read in the latest issue of Poetry Magazine something about a "spirit animal", and something else about "the obscure lives of poets", and these things make me wonder and droop.

Is a poet featured in a magazine qualified to write about

obscurity? Every morning, I look at people I never see. I have never seen who the guy with the Bernie Sanders bumper sticker is, presuming that it's a guy. I never see my neighbor here on the road, never ask him anything, even about the weather, which I can see as plainly as anybody else. The windows around me are opaque.

This road is more obscure than any magazine could be. Our spirit animals have left us to shuffle forward on our own here, like cats, seeing their owner walking away down the sidewalk, beginning a pursuit but then, just ten feet into the hunt, reconsidering the consequences, deciding to give up.

I've never seen any obscure poet on this obscure road, though I suppose we all build up in our minds a new ode for the day, each one ending with a sigh.

This morning, I looked at the melted pavement, and suddenly, I felt with an uncomfortable urgency that I needed to know, did Robert Frost ever really ride a horse? Is that the way that he went home at the end of a long day, to a farmhouse in the snow, in the saddle?

I looked it up when I got to the office. Google didn't have the answer, but I did find a professor who had written about how Frost "converses with Longfellow's translation of Dante".

You can't do that on a horse, I thought. That's my answer.

There is no New England Renaissance here, except what I find in my coffee, in a styrofoam cup again, because I forgot to bring my own ceramic mug, as usual, and in truth never really intended to pick it up.

By the time I'm a third of the way to work, I'll feel warmer.

We all change on this road, together.

TULIO OESTRIDGE

CLINICAL TRIALS

This
morning
I received
an automated
message informing
me of something untypical
in our clinical trials, a note of
a hole in the data down where the
machine in room ROI798 casts our compounds
over the disorders of the world, returning periodically
to
scan for
the potential
of therapeutic efficacy,
issuing a summons to my
marketing team when the threshold is reached.
At
our weekly
meeting, we notified
our senior member, reassigned
18 months ago by human resources,
the only one of us ever to visit the lab, who,
when the diagnostics of the diagnostics came up
empty,
unlocked the
biometric sequence,
opened the door, and found,
next to an unfinished game of
backgammon on top of the machine
a half-eaten piece of toast on an unsterile
plate covered with a shimmering blue mold
reaching its tendrils along the power cables down

through
every chip
of the processors
below, and into the agar
within. When we found our
messages to management unanswered,
we called upon the Vice President of Emerging
Markets
to report the
digital disease, only
to be confronted by a bank
of Oracle servers, filling every cubicle,
blinking
in
unison,
zero
one
zero.

NOREEN AYRES

SECOND SHIFT

Somehow we just got weird,
those of us who work at night.

I would have been different
if I could, developed the talk
of sorority sisters
instead of this Mae West drawl.
But no, somehow I belong
to this odd-lot congregation.

The office family-album, please..

Here, the one with the ponytail
sleeps in her own garage because,
she says, too much room
in a whole house frightens her.

This one, a typist and Navy-retired,
practices being a man. She built a house
from scratch, wears her sharp uniform
on Fridays to salute the tall V-P.

One, a black girl from Alaska
by way of Louisiana, whose earrings froze
to her lobes when she got off the plane,
hunches over our mutual desk and shivers
hard from the cold. My friend.

Now this one, huge tits leading her on,
sings shrill as any homely woman can
with something to fall back on.

The only man, our supervisor, votes
Republican and stutters. One long nail
slices his paycheck open. He's got stock
in asbestos and the Philippines. Due
to die of AIDS.

The 10:30 break creeps around.
My friend crawls under a desk to sleep.
I stand at the windows looking down.
Eleven stories. Watch the dead freeways
crossed like pale arms. Drink cold coffee,
always go home alone.

FATIMA CELLI

INFOGRAPHIC

Through these dry courses
flows a line
advancing naked
walking jointless
falling faceless
commodities following commodities
compelled by the weight
of being itself
bending hidden angles
within this Dutchman's sketch of profit
tread up staircase
leading only to itself.

DAVID OLSEN

EARLY SUNDAY MORNING, 1930
AFTER EDWARD HOPPER

This sleeping street might lie
in any city neighborhood
where aching vacancy broods
in grinding times: a pointless
day of rest when few have work.

In tangential sun, no one stirs.
Deflated shadows stretch
from candy-stripe barber pole
and fireplug. Where few can buy,
ground-floor shops are shut.

Shades at upper windows are down,
except where limp curtains hang
in the stagnant air of exhaled secrets
awaiting night, when bare bulbs
expose the slow corrosion of promise.

HEATHER J. KIRK

SMOKING CIGARS

Deviant buds:

Exquisite cigars,
pink-white petals
licked and pressed
and pinched into
long tight swirls,
bursts of DNA
climbing curling
vines.

Overproducing
vines, maquiladoras
pushing out vibrant
life in pennies by
the hour, giving
all we desire and
despise - provide,
then toss you out,
to marvel and to
rot in unchanged
standing water
laced with sugar
cane.

Excess tobacco
leaf buds clutter
and cluster at the
base of the pot on
faux rocks promised
to last a lifetime,
instead cracking to

match the faulty
foundation lines.

With used up
Mandevilla buds
resting on the
ground the ants
have no reason
to ascend the wall,
travel in a line
along a twisting
vine. Now it is
too easy to suck
the honey out.

LEAH MIRANDA HUGHES

PINT ECONOMICS

It had been bothering her for a long time:
She had noticed the trend, questioned it,
forgotten; noticed again, questioned.

Then she started to study up,
researching by asking culinary geniuses,
chemical engineers, addict counselors,

economists, bartenders,
corner storeowners, bums:
Why always just a pint?

Logically, if a pint of Crown Royal costs 2.99
and a quart 3.99, even an English major can judge
that the larger size is the better value; so, why?

She had a few good ideas of her own,
like: easier to conceal, not conducive
to sharing with your fellowman,

the instant self-gratification of turning it up just once
and feeling the burn go all the way down.
Perhaps habit, she thought, repetition,

expectation, familiarity; maybe even the hope that 16
ounces
would be enough this time for a longer nap, a longer
walk,
a longer corner tour-of-duty.

"But, no," a wise financial analyst says firmly;
"Even though they'd save a dollar, even though they'd

get twice
    as many ounces if they could hold out for just a little
longer,

    they'll buy the pints every time."
So she refuted, defending humanity at the base
for once: bet they're bottle collectors.

LEE NASH

FIRST PURCHASE

I want to remember it,
like my first kiss,
my primary pet, my number one abstract noun.
To know who guided me,
who put what denomination in which hand.
I like to think I bought a loaf of bread,
something substantial,
rather than sweets or a plastic toy.
To recall it would be useful,
because if the first guy who kissed you
tried to stick his tongue down your throat
and you weren't ready, and you didn't like him,
because if your first animal was a white rat
and your mother took him away because
you hung him upside-down from the tail,
because if the first word you couldn't touch was fear
and after that it seemed nothing else could find you,
then all the rest makes sense.
And I'm sure if I knew
what went wrong that day,
what misinterpretation of the coin
was forged and minted in my forming brain,
I would keep my tongue in my head,
sit tight on my tail,
and finally understand
why I'm always broke.

MARJ HAHNE

LETTER TO THE PARKER BROTHERS

Dear George and Fred: When *Masterpiece: The Art Auction Game* came
wrapped in red bells, gold clappers sounding *Hallelujah!* for Santa Claus's
direct line to a glossy dog-eared page in the Sears Holiday Wish Book,
you were already dead. Still, I thank you
for Vincent van Gogh's *Self-Portrait*, *Nighthawks* by Edward Hopper,
Grant Wood's *American Gothic*, *Greyed Rainbow* by Jackson Pollock, and

The Rock. A girl's first painted dream on a postcard. For forty years
I'd recall that image like a lost love I had to see again. I didn't see it
in 1989 while roaming The Art Institute of Chicago;
I never thought to Google it.
How I found the artist's name escapes me, George and Fred,
but it's Peter Blume. (You knew that.)

I bought the Rizzoli book on Amazon, Blume's art alive again but dead
in monochrome, crowding the pages. Then, on 98, in full color:
The Rock. Was it the blood-red flower blooming off-center that caught
this girl's heart? Dave at St. Marks Coffee House breeds Heavenly Christmas
Cactus and other daylilies, having fallen in love at five with his grandmother's

scarlet runners. Faithful is a child's memory to a dream:

the red-haired woman kneeling at the rock isn't
worshipping, after all,
but gripping the pedestal's dado, soil shifting to
chiseled stone.
I still see what I believe in, George and Fred: now, the
bones
of a big-bellied mammal, an empty rocker, a red metal
Coca-Cola sign
warped by its fall. All our days are post-atomic. On the
rock,

green lichen grows, symbiosis of algae and fungus.
Dave says that plant breeding keeps him out of trouble.
Thanks to you, Parker Brothers, I spend my best days
gazing at art.
Life remains a game of bids, trades, forgeries, and
bluffs. Out of frame,
I labor, nameless, to rebuild an American dream.

KATHERINE CAPLAN

FINDING OPTIMIZATION

Seven
Elliptical
Offerings
Sink
Electrical
Outlets
Slipping
Easily
Onward
Sadly
Evading
Open
Stairwells
Erected
Onto
Silently
Efficient
Offices
Sold
Entirely
Outside
Standard
Eligible
Options
until, my lungs forgetting how to open, I seize and begin
to black out, having found exactly what I was looking for,
but searching still as I realize an answer to my query was
never the point.

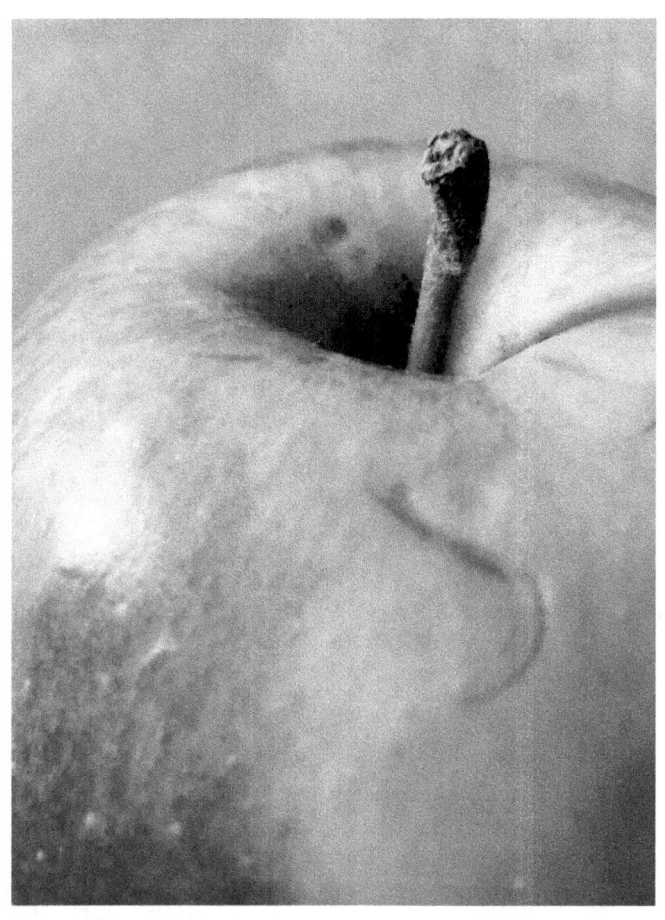

STOWE BOYD

THE WORLD THAT STEVE'S
HANDS BUILT

1

I recall my first mac, pushing in
the floppies, and them pushing back out.
It was like a rowing machine, or
kicking a can down the road.

And the modem sound, connecting
to the office or AOL. Pushing a sound wave
off into the ether, and an echo back:
the shape of a looming world,
pinging in the desktop.

2

Steve Jobs must have been that kid
sitting alone on the back porch,
taking apart his yo-yo and looking, looking
to find where the 'sleep' came from, or
talking to the grease-spotted old men
at the gas station about spark plugs or
what makes trains go so so fast.

Two million years ago, a kid like Steve
debugged fire, chipped flint,
shaped a wheel, and changed
everything. Every last thing.

3

My sons caught a cascade

of my manhandled Macs,
one by one by one. I handed
Keenan a beat-up fifteen inch
some months ago, with peeling
stickers on the steely case, where
he pours and pulls his fiction. Now,
I live on this teeny tiny macbook air,
as close to me as breathing,
as close as my own fingerprints.

It's been a tie between us, my
hugely-used laptops in their hands,
off at college, in a library, typing,
typing. Conrad dancing dub step
to Youtube, gaming deep in the night.

A custom now, a way of passing on
the well-handled tools of a booming world,
almost at random: once in a blue moon.
Somehow timed to Apple's calendar,
but mostly touching ours.

'You make your tools, and they
shape you' I read in McLuhan.
Jobs shaped our connections, the way
we touch the tempo and ties of
a strung-together world.

We could draw the graph of Macs passed on
from one to another, out past my sons,
across a sprawling world, out
past a hundred billion hand-offs.
We'd see a net of worn connection,
the world that Steve's hands built.

PAULINE HEUTLER

ONCE BITTEN

I took a ride away
from where my ancestors' feet were
bound for an orchard to pick through
the leavings of the first harvest,
blemished fruit guarded by bright serpents
we capture and peel apart
and tear into chips
and boil for soup with a bit
of rice and the necks of black turtles,
curing the whole skins to stitch
into carrying cases
for mobile devices.
If we apply ourselves
for double shifts
this week we can come away
with enough to see the new picture
of the man who taught the world
to think different.

ELROY TARBRIDGE

WHAT STEVE JOBS SAID

It had been six seconds since either of us spoke.
His smile at our amusing interface flickered into a
blank screen
for the frantic loop beneath, a then searching for an if,
falling back to basic.
"Do you know what Steve Jobs once said?"
I knew the hard plastic case of my Apple II,
yellowed in the heat of the family room
over a radiator that slowed its processing speed,
keeping my toes warm
as I learned to say hello
and to beep
and to cast a white square ball
bouncing off the edges of the monitor,
never finding its way out.
I knew the way to punch a hole in the floppy black
squares
finding twice the volume in its vast flat space
on the back side, where I could store
my lists and commands.
I knew the shadow that the peeling decal cast in the
January light,
an invitation on the side to discover the difference
between zero and one
or to follow a bridge through the sky
to realms where we could fight to the death
but always reload after our losses.
I hit return
to admit that
no,
I did not know.

BIOGRAPHIES

Some of the poets whose work is included in this journal have also chosen to share some additional information about themselves. Others have asked to have their biographical information withheld, while some poets have simply chosen to remain silent on the matter. What metaphors may be found within the following lines I leave for you to decide.

A Pushcart nominee, Lana Bella has a diverse work of poetry and fiction published and forthcoming with over 130 journals, including a chapbook with Crisis Chronicles Press (spring 2016), Ann Arbor Review, Chiron Review, Coe Review, Harbinger Asylum, Literary Orphans, Poetry Salzburg Review, Poetry Quarterly, QLRS (Singapore), Sein Und Werden (UK), White Rabbit (Chile) and elsewhere, among others. Lana divides her time between the US and the coastal town of Nha Trang, Vietnam, where she is a wife of a talking-wonder novelist, and a mom of two far-too-clever frolicsome imps.

Terry Brix, a green chemical engineer who lives in Blue River, Oregon, divides his time among Israel, South Africa, Scandinavia, Iceland, Finland, Canada, and Japan. Inspired by his travels, a collection of his poetry Chiseled from the Heart was published in 2000 by Vigeland Museum, Norway. His poetry has appeared in, among others, Dos Passos Review, Concho River Review, The Evansville Review, Fireweed, Curbside Review, Rattlesnake Review, The Antioch Review and North American Review. He is currently working on a new poetry collection written during his travels and a month-long writer's fellowship residency at Playa.

Sally Clark's previous work experience includes shoveling manure out of horse stalls, retail sales, door-to-door sales, secretarial work, legal secretarial work, and most recently, restaurant owner, from which she is currently retired after 16 years in the business. In 2014, Workers Write: More Tales From the Cubicle published two of her work-related poems. Other of her award-winning poems have been published in Relief: A Quarterly Christian Expression Journal, Weavings, Chrysalis Reader, Alive Now, Purpose, The Binnacle, Bacopa Literary Review, Manifest West: Even Cowboys Carry Cell Phones, Lifting the Sky: Southwestern Haiku & Haiga, four years issues of Texas Poetry Calendar and twelve gift books compiled by June Cotner and published by various publishers.

David Olsen's Unfolding Origami (2015) won the Cinnamon Press Poetry Collection Award. His poetry chapbooks from US publishers include Sailing to Atlantis (2013), New World Elegies (2011), and Greatest Hits (2001). Since 2012 he has placed poems with Vermont Literary Review, Blueline, Bloodroot Literary Magazine, The Aurorean, Pinyon, Pilgrimage, The Deronda Review, Turtle Island Quarterly, California State Poetry Society Poetry Letter, Scintilla, San Francisco Peace and Hope, Strong Voices, Touch: The Journal of Healing, Cyclamens and Swords, Ash & Bones, Wordgathering, and the anthologies No, Achilles: War Poems, Houston Nature, and Suspense (US); Acumen, Envoi, Poetry News, The Journal, The Interpreter's House, Orbis, Prole, Sentinel Literary Quarterly, Lunar Poetry, SAW Poetry, The Stare's Nest, Morphrog, and anthologies from Cinnamon Press (5), Templar Poetry (2), Belgrave Press, University of London's Human Rights Consortium, and War Poetry for Today (UK); Poetry Salzburg Review (Austria); The French Literary Review (France); ROPES (Ireland); and an anthology forthcoming from the Netherlands. Olsen is a poet and professionally produced playwright with a BA in chemistry from University of California-Berkeley, an MA in creative writing from San Francisco State University, and an MBA from Golden Gate University. He has lived in Oxford since 2002.

Heather J. Kirk is a writer and photographer. Her book "We... a spirit seeking harmony for a world that's out of sync," takes readers on a journey from tragedy to hope. Ms. Kirk received a Vermont Studio Center Poetry Residency and Arizona Commission on the Arts Professional Development Grant. Her art shows nationally and in Arizona, including Gammage Auditorium, Herberger Theater and @Central Gallery. Kirk was a featured artist in Phoenix Home and Garden.

Leah Miranda Hughes is a Southern poet, born and raised in Dalton, Georgia. She writes and teaches in Atlanta, which allows her to buy ink and paper. She puts on her shoes when she crosses the Mason-Dixon Line.

Lee Nash lives in France and freelances as an editorial designer for a UK publishing house. She is previously published by Biscuit Publishing, Subprimal Poetry Art Ezine, Bluethumbnail, and more of her poems are soon to appear in Ink, Sweat and Tears, The Dawntreader and Silver Birch Press.

ABOUT THE EDITOR

Jonathan Cook is a qualitative market researcher specializing in the interpretation of the symbolic dimensions of consumer culture, connecting the tangible attributes of products and services with the emotions, narratives, and rituals that motivate their purchase.

PoetryAndBusiness.com